Top of the Table

Chris Powling
Illustrated by Jon Stuart

Chapter 1 – Leo's idea

Max, Kat, Leo, and Jet were in Leo's bedroom.

Max was looking out of the window. "A storm is on its way."

"A storm?" said Kat.

"I can't believe it," said Jet. "Today of all days!"

The Greenville School team was supposed to play the most important match of the season that afternoon.

"If we beat Woodside School, we'll be at the top of the league table," said Kat. "We'll be this year's champions!"

"Not unless the weather clears up, you won't," said Leo.

Jet groaned.

Gloomily, they stared out at the sky. It had never looked so grim and gray.

Max tried to cheer them up. "If the storm breaks, we'll be able to play."

Leo had an idea. "Hey!" he exclaimed. "Why don't we play a soccer match in here?"

"In here?" Kat frowned.

"I was thinking of *table* soccer," said Leo.

Chapter 2 – Bad tempers

Leo was easily the best player. He rotated the poles and moved the players like an expert. Max was nearly as good. It was Kat and Jet who couldn't get the hang of it. Kat kept missing the ball, and Jet kept twisting his players the wrong way.

Soon Max and Leo were winning 5–0. Kat and Jet were furious.

"Kat, you're hopeless!" Jet snapped. "Your players spend more time missing the ball than kicking it."

"Well, how many goals have *you* scored?" she answered back.

Max and Leo sighed.

"If this were a real game, I'd easily beat you," said Kat.

"Yeah, right!" laughed Jet.

"Why not find out?" said Leo, with a grin.

"It's raining, remember?" said Kat.

"I don't think Leo expects you to go outside," explained Max.

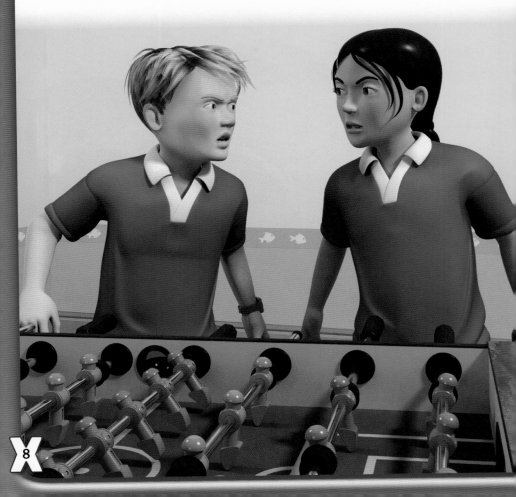

"Shrink to micro-size," said Leo. "Let's see how good you really are!"

Kat and Jet turned the dials on their watches and . . .

Chapter 3 – The shoot-out

Leo's idea was to have a penalty shoot-out. Kat and Jet would take turns and get five shots each. Leo would work the plastic goalie.

"The one who scores the most goals will be the winner," Max explained. "I'll be the referee."

"I'm bound to be the winner!" Jet boasted.
Jet placed the ball on the penalty spot.

Max blew a whistle. Jet ran toward the ball. He kicked it hard, but he didn't score. The plastic goalie stopped the ball—with a tap from Leo.

"Move over," said Kat. "This is how it's done."

Kat put the ball on the spot. Max blew his whistle. Kat aimed carefully, kicking hard. Again, the plastic goalie stopped the ball— with a flick from Leo.

Kat and Jet each had four more shots left.
They tried again and again to score a goal, but Leo was just too good at controlling the goalie.

Then, on the fourth attempt, both Kat and Jet managed to score a goal each.

They now had one shot left to decide who would be the winner.

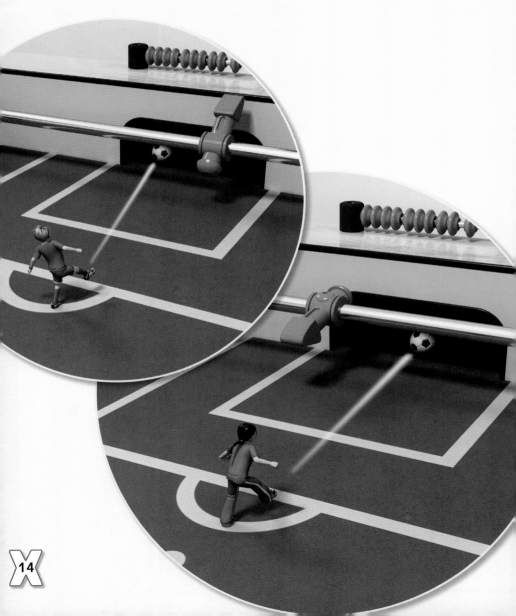

Chapter 4 – The last penalty

Max's heart sank. OK, so one of them might win the penalty shoot-out, but how would the other one feel?

Jet placed the ball carefully on the penalty spot. It was the last of his five shots. Max blew his whistle.

A moment later Max could barely believe his eyes. Jet had messed up his shot. The ball only barely reached the goal-line.

Jet slumped on the table. "I'm supposed to be Greenville School's best striker," he wailed. "I can't even beat a plastic goalie!"

Kat looked at Jet suspiciously.

She placed the ball on the penalty spot and waited for the sound of Max's whistle.

Kat's last penalty kick wasn't much better than Jet's. The ball ended up a long way outside of the goal area.

"Oops," said Kat.

"Hey!" said Jet. "That wasn't a real kick. You messed it up on purpose!"

"So did you!" Kat answered back.

"I didn't want you to get upset," said Jet,
more softly.

"I didn't want *you* to get upset," said Kat.
"After all, we are on the same team."

Leo bent over the two tiny figures on the tabletop. "Congratulations," he beamed, "you're finally getting along!"

"Hey, look!" shouted Max, pointing out of the window. "The sky is clearing. Greenville will be playing Woodside after all! You had better get back to normal size."

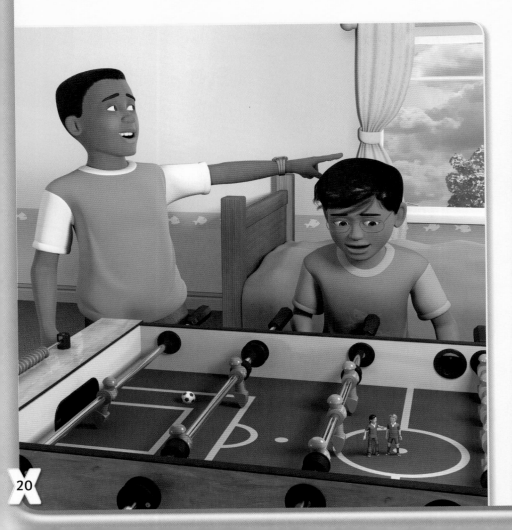

Chapter 5 – Champions

The score was 1–0. Woodside School was in the lead.

Kat weaved in and out of the players as she ran down the field. She saw her chance. The Woodside School goalie was standing to one side of the goal.

Kat kicked the ball into the other corner of the net. Greenville School let out a huge cry! It was 1–1.

One minute before the end of the game, Kat passed the ball to Jet. Jet took a shot at the goal, but a player from Woodside School tripped him. The referee blew his whistle. Foul!

The referee handed the ball to Jet to take a free penalty kick.

This was Greenville's chance to win the game. Jet carefully placed the ball on the penalty spot. He kicked the ball as hard as he could— right past Woodside's goalie. It landed in the net! Greenville had won.

Greenville School team gathered around Mrs. Mills, the principal.

"Without you two we wouldn't be at the top of the league table!" she smiled. "Have you had some sort of special training?"

"Well, sort of . . . " said Kat.

"Yeah . . . with a little help from some friends," said Jet, waving to Leo and Max.